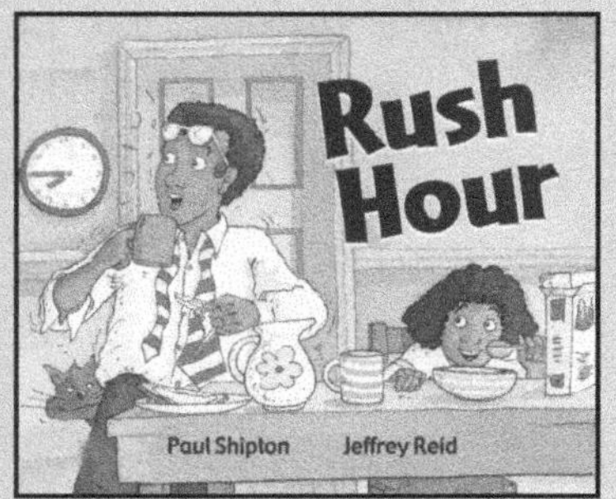

Walkthrough

Do you sometimes have to rush to get to school in the morning?

Do you ever forget things?

This story is called 'Rush Hour'.

Why do you think the story is called 'Rush Hour'?

Walkthrough

Let's read the blurb together.

Do you ever have to help your parents in the early morning rush?

What sort of things do you do?

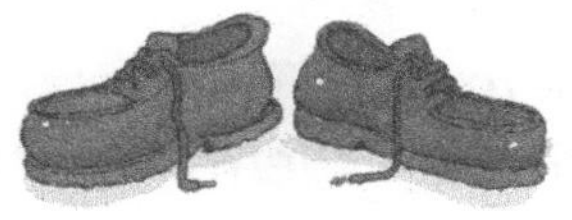

Walkthrough

Let's read the title: 'Rush Hour'.

What can you see in the picture?

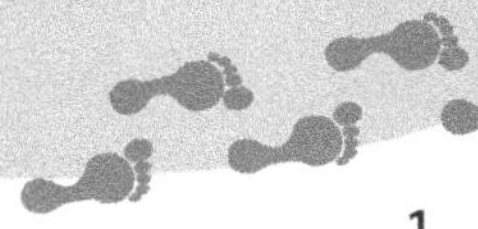

2

Observe and Prompt

Word Recognition

- Check the children can read the adjacent consonants at the end of 'books'.

- Check the children can read the words 'Where' and 'There' using their decoding skills. You may need to help them with the 'ere' sound if they struggle.

- Check the children can read 'chair' using their decoding skills. You may need to help them with the 'air' sound if they struggle.

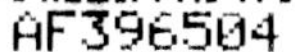

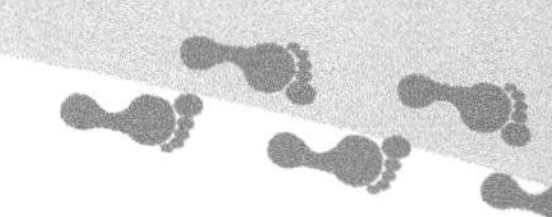

3

3

What is Dad looking for here?

What do you think he says?

Who has found them?

What do you think the girl is saying?

"Now I can't find my sandwiches.
Where are they?" asked Dad.

4

Observe and Prompt

Word Recognition

- Check the children can read the adjacent consonants at the end of 'find'.

- If the children have difficulty with the word 'sandwiches', prompt them to break it down into three syllables – 'sand', 'wich' and 'es', before blending the whole word together.

- Check the children can read the 'ed' suffix in the word 'asked'.

- If the children have difficulty with the word 'fridge', model the blending of this word for them.

"Here they are, in the
fridge," I said.

5

Language Comprehension

- Ask the children what Dad can't find now.
- Where do the children think his sandwiches are?
- Ask the children what the little girl says to her Dad.
- How do the children think Dad feels?

What's Dad looking for now?

Where is he looking?

How do you think Dad feels?

What do you think the girl is saying?

"Where are my keys?"
asked Dad.

6

 **Observe and Prompt**

Word Recognition

- Check the children can read 'keys' using their decoding skills. You may need to help them with the 'ey' sound if this has not yet been taught.

- Check the children can read 'Here'. If they have difficulty, model the blending of this word for them.

- Check the children can read 'table'. Help them with the vowel sound and 'le' ending if they have difficulty.

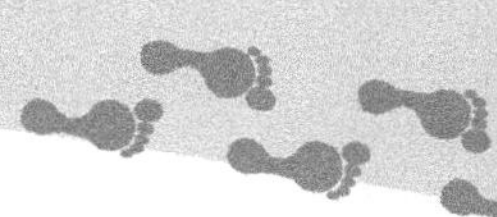

"Here they are, on the
table," I said.

7

Language Comprehension

- Observe that the children have established the text pattern.
- Ask the children what Dad says.
- Where do the children think his keys are?
- What do the children think Dad will look for next?

Walkthrough

Now Dad says he is late.

What else does he need to find?

Where are his bags?

Observe and Prompt

Word Recognition

- Check the children can read 'Now' using their decoding skills. Help them with the 'ow' sound if necessary.

- If the children have difficulty reading 'late', help them with the 'ay' sound.

- If the children have difficulty reading 'cupboard', model the reading of this word for them.

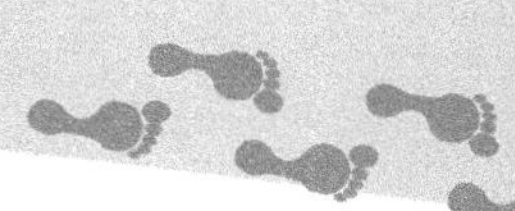

"In the cupboard, Dad," I said.

9

 **Observe and Prompt**

Language Comprehension

- Ask the children what Dad says now. What is he looking for?
- How do the children think Dad feels?
- Ask the children who finds Dad's bags. Where are they?
- Do the children think Dad will have lost anything else?

Walkthrough

What's Dad looking for now?

What might he say?

How do you think the girl feels about Dad
losing things?

 **Observe and Prompt**

Word Recognition

- If the children are having difficulty reading 'gloves', model
  the blending of this word for them.

- Check the children can read 'drawer' using their decoding
  skills. If they have difficulty, help them with the 'aw' sound.

10

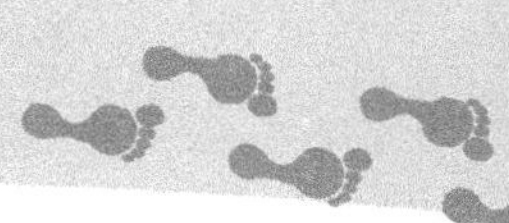

"Oh Dad! They are in the
drawer," I said.

11

 **Observe and Prompt**

Language Comprehension

- Ask the children what Dad can't find now.
- Where do the children think his gloves are?
- Do the children think Dad will get to work on time?
- What else do the children think he might have lost?

Walkthrough

What has Dad lost now?

What might the girl tell him?

What time is it now?

12

 **Observe and Prompt**

Word Recognition

- Check the children can read 'pens' and 'pocket' using their decoding skills.

- Check the children can read 'be'.

- Help the children with the word 'your' if they struggle.

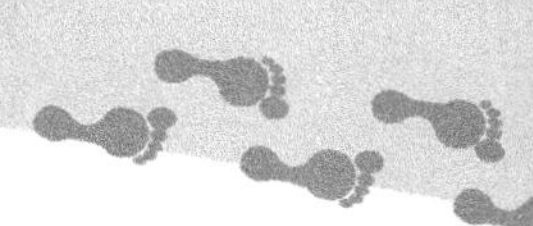

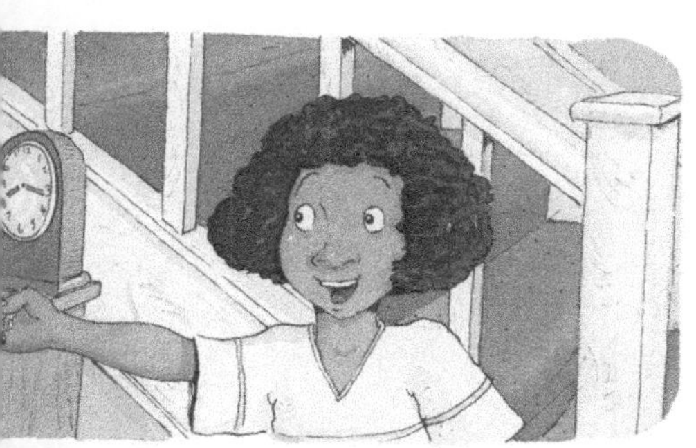

"In your pocket," I said.

13

Language Comprehension

- Ask the children what Dad asks this time.
- Ask the children what the little girl says to her Dad.
- Do the children think Dad is ready to go to work now?

Where's Dad going?

Has he got everything?

What does he remember?

What do you think the girl says?

How does Dad feel?

 **Observe and Prompt**

Word Recognition

- If the children have difficulty reading 'glasses', model the blending of this word for them.

- Check the children can read 'head'. Help the children with the 'ea' sound if they struggle.

"On your head," I said.

15

 **Observe and Prompt**

Language Comprehension

- Observe the children reading with expression.
- Ask the children what Dad has lost now.
- Ask the children where his glasses are.
- Do the children think Dad will forget anything else?

Walkthrough

What has Dad forgotten?

What do you think the girl says?

Turn back to the title page – are these Dad's shoes?

 **Observe and Prompt**

Word Recognition

- Check the children can read 'shoes' using their decoding skills. You may need to help them with the 'oe' sound if you have not yet taught this phoneme.

Language Comprehension

- Observe expressive reading. If necessary, point out the exclamation mark.
- Ask the children what Dad has forgotten now?
- Ask the children what the little girl says to her Dad.